THE BLUE MARBLE

HOW A PHOTOGRAPH REVEALED EARTH'S FRAGILE BEAUTY

by Don Nardo

Content Adviser: James Gerard
NASA Education Specialist
Kennedy Space Center

COMPASS POINT BOOKS
a capstone imprint

Compass Point Books are published by Capstone,
1710 Roe Crest Drive, North Mankato, Minnesota 56003
www.capstonepub.com

Editor: Catherine Neitge
Designer: Tracy Davies McCabe
Media Researcher: Svetlana Zhurkin
Library Consultant: Kathleen Baxter
Production Specialist: Kathy McColley

Image Credits
Corbis: Bettmann, 48; DVIDS: NASA, 39, 42, 47, 55; NASA, 5, 6, 7, 10, 25, 27,
28, 31, 32, 36, 38, 45, 58 (left), 59 (top), Earth Observatory/NOAA/DOD, 51, 59
(bottom), Johnson Space Center, cover, 12, 41, 58 (right), JPL, 30, Kennedy Space
Center, 35, NOAA, 53, NOAA/GSFC/Suomi NPP/VIIRS/Norman Kuring, 52; Newscom:
akg-images, 23, akg-images/Peter Connolly, 18, ZUMA Press/Sudres Jean-Daniel, 16;
Shutterstock: catwalker, 50, Iryna1, 22, 57 (top), Panos Karas, 20, 56; Wikimedia:
Department of Defense Gravitational Experiment, 8, U.S. Air Force, 15, 57 (bottom)

Library of Congress Cataloging-in-Publication Data
Nardo, Don, 1947– author.
  The blue marble: how a photograph revealed Earth's fragile beauty / by Don Nardo.
  pages cm.—(Compass point books. Captured history)
  Summary: "Discusses the iconic Blue Marble photo of Earth taken by the Apollo 17
astronauts in December 1972"—Provided by publisher.
  Audience: 10-14.
  Audience: Grades 4 to 6.
  Includes bibliographical references and index.
  ISBN 978-0-7565-4732-5 (library binding)
  ISBN 978-0-7565-4788-2 (paperback)
ISBN 978-0-7565-4794-3 (ebook PDF)
1. Earth (Planet)—Photographs from space—Juvenile literature. 2. Apollo 17
(Spacecraft)—Juvenile literature. 3. Photographs—History—Juvenile literature.
I. Title. II. Series: Captured history.
  QL737.C2N37 2014
  525.022'2—dc23   2013031184

Printed in the United States of America in Stevens Point, Wisconsin.
092013   007773WZS14

TABLEOFCONTENTS

Chapter One

A PIECE OF BLUE IN SPACE

"We're not the first to discover this, but we'd like to confirm ... that the world is round." These words from Eugene Cernan, commander of the *Apollo 17* spacecraft, reached Mission Control on Earth in less than a second. The men and women monitoring the mission that day— December 7, 1972—smiled at Cernan's little joke. Humor was welcome because it helped to break the tension they were naturally feeling at that moment.

The *Apollo 17* craft had launched from NASA's John F. Kennedy Space Center on Florida's eastern coast five hours before. Everyone involved was concentrating hard on doing their jobs. Their goal was to place Cernan and another astronaut on the moon's surface. There they would travel farther than any of the U.S. astronauts who had walked on the moon. They would do so using NASA's Lunar Roving Vehicle. The LRV, which weighed 460 pounds (209 kilograms), was similar to a golf cart but much more sophisticated. It would allow the astronauts to explore the surface out to a distance of 6 miles (9.7 kilometers) from the landing craft. (The LRV could go farther. But to be on the safe side, mission planners had restricted the trips to 6 miles to conserve the men's oxygen and other elements of life support.)

While exploring, the astronauts would collect soil and rock samples. Studying these materials on Earth would

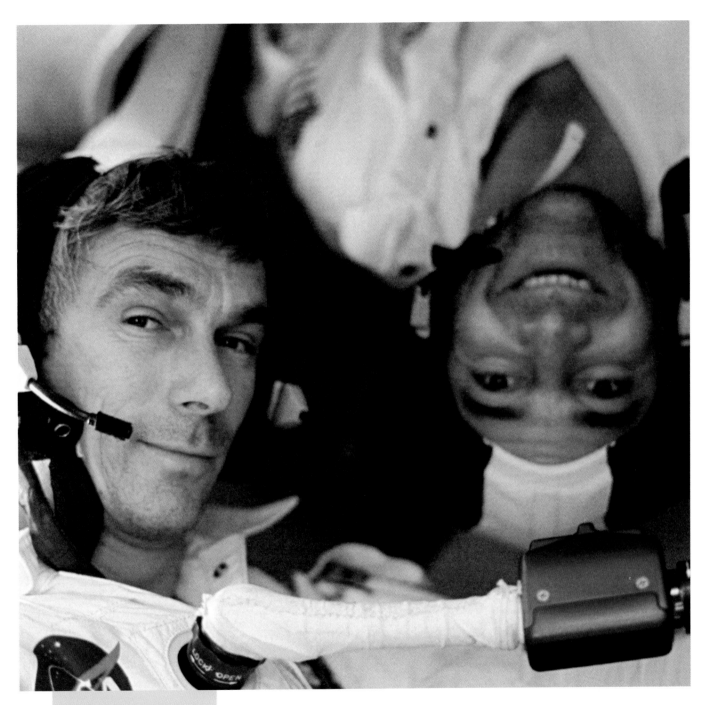

help scientists determine the moon's physical makeup and age. They might also be able to figure out how the moon had formed.

When NASA was planning the mission, no one foresaw that there would be a huge bonus. Even as he quipped about Earth's being round, Cernan was unaware that *Apollo 17* would soon produce an iconic photo. This stunning image would show planet Earth as a lonely globe floating in the inky black immenseness of outer space. Nicknamed "the Blue Marble," the picture was destined to become a good deal more famous than the mission itself.

Schmitt is convinced he shot the famous Blue Marble photo.

Within a few years it would achieve the reputation of being one of the most often reproduced and most recognizable photos in history.

Considering the picture's almost legendary status, it is perhaps surprising that it still is not clear which of the three *Apollo 17* crewmen took it. Besides the commander, Eugene Cernan, command module pilot Ronald Evans and Harrison "Jack" Schmitt, the lunar module pilot and mission geologist, were on board.

Schmitt later said he snapped the shot in question.

A communications satellite photographed Earth in 1967 with a black and white TV camera. Three photos, each with a red, green, or blue filter, created the color image. The small disk in front is a color match card.

Whoever actually snapped the renowned photo, it was not the first one taken of Earth's completely illuminated disk.

"I treasure the whole mission," he said in a 2012 interview. "Every day had more than one really spectacular event. The first day, we saw this nearly full Earth, and I was able to take that picture [the Blue Marble], still the most requested photograph in the NASA archives."

NASA officials who studied the mission data agreed that Schmitt was most likely the photo's creator. But they found that all three astronauts had taken images of Earth on their first day in space. And they were not paying strict attention to who was taking which photo. So the officials could not determine the Blue Marble's photographer with certainty. To be fair, therefore, the official credit for the picture went to the entire *Apollo 17* crew.

Whoever actually snapped the renowned photo, it was not the first one taken of Earth's completely illuminated disk. Cameras mounted on a satellite had already captured such shots. In 1967, two years before U.S. astronauts (on the *Apollo 11* mission) first landed on the moon, NASA's ATS-3 communications satellite had taken photos of Earth's full disk.

Earlier astronauts had also seen and photographed one side of Earth from space. The *Apollo 8* spacecraft had made history December 24, 1968, as the first manned spacecraft to orbit the moon. At one point its crewmen caught sight of Earth appearing to rise above the lunar horizon.

Later dubbed "Earthrise," the photo taken during the *Apollo 8* mission became almost as iconic as the Blue

A SUPERB SPECTACLE

Earthrise, photographed Christmas Eve 1968, was the first color photo of Earth taken by a person from lunar orbit.

Surprisingly, when planning the *Apollo 8* mission in 1968, NASA officials did not prepare the astronauts for an "Earthrise," as seen from the moon. So the three crewmen were taken off guard when they saw it. "Oh my God!" mission commander Frank Borman exclaimed. "Look at that picture over there! Here's the Earth coming up. Wow, is that pretty!" Jim Lovell agreed: "Oh man, that's great!"

After frantically loading a camera with color film, their crewmate, William Anders, aimed his camera out a window. Carefully, he snapped a shot of the superb spectacle of a gibbous Earth hanging in the lunar sky.

Marble. The main difference between the two was the coverage of the planet's surface. The Blue Marble, taken from an altitude of about 28,000 miles (45,000 km), showed a full Earth rather than a gibbous Earth. (*Gibbous* refers to the phase in which a planet or moon is more than half but not fully illuminated.) The sun was directly behind the *Apollo 17* spacecraft. So its occupants were able to create the first image of a fully lit side of Earth from space.

Much of the 1972 *Apollo 17* image was a deep blue, mostly created by sunlight reflecting off the Atlantic and Indian oceans. It was accented by the warm brown hue of Africa and other landmasses. There were also bold streaks of white, some from clouds but more from gleaming ice sheets in Antarctica, the ice-covered continent at the South Pole. The photo's mix of colors, combined with the shininess of the disk in the brilliant sunlight, reminded those who first saw it of a glass marble. That is the origin of the name Blue Marble. Moved by the sight, Schmitt said, "If there ever was a fragile-appearing piece of blue in space, it's the Earth right now."

The planet's delicate, frail quality probably was one factor that made the photo so popular worldwide. The early 1970s was an era of environmental awareness and activism. Many Americans were awakening to an important reality—that hurting the environment in one region affects people's lives in

"If there ever was a fragile-appearing piece of blue in space, it's the Earth right now."

other regions. The idea that all humans are passengers on a spaceship called Earth was becoming increasingly evident and accepted.

American biochemist Gregory A. Petsko summed it up beautifully. In the Blue Marble image, he wrote, the entire planet appeared "tiny, vulnerable, and incredibly lonely against the vast blackness of the cosmos. It also seemed whole in a way that no map could illustrate. Regional conflict and petty differences could be dismissed as trivial compared with environmental dangers that threatened all of humanity, traveling together through the void on this fragile-looking marble."

ChapterTwo
DREAMERS OF WHAT MIGHT BE

The creation of the historic Blue Marble and Earthrise photos was possible only because the age of space flight was under way. In 1957 the Russian satellite *Sputnik 1* became the first human-made object to orbit Earth. Its flight shocked and fascinated the world, in large part because many people seemed to assume space travel was impossible. Feats like photographing Earth from space and landing on the moon and planets happened only in science fiction stories.

During the many centuries before these space exploits, only a tiny handful of people in each generation thought such things were possible. Well before scientific advances *made* them possible, they dreamed big and passed their enthusiasm on to others. Such fascination and zeal for what humans might someday achieve helped to fuel the curiosity of early creative thinkers, in a sense the first scientists. Little by little they made the necessary and crucial discoveries. For example, they showed that Earth is a sphere and later proved that it revolves around the sun. Later still they figured out how gravity works and how to build rockets to escape its grasp.

Thus the Blue Marble, the moon landings, and other major achievements in space exploration did not happen by accident. They were the result of many centuries of slow but steady scientific progress. And they could not

Feats like photographing Earth from space and landing on the moon and planets happened only in science fiction stories.

Sputnik 1, from a Russian word that means *co-traveler*, was about the size of a beach ball.

have happened without the contributions of those few intrepid dreamers of what might be.

The identities of the earliest of those visionaries are lost. Perhaps the first was a spear-carrying hunter-gatherer roaming through the wilderness of what is now Africa. Or possibly he or she lived in the Middle East or Europe. There is no doubt that the early natives of those regions had a strong interest in the night sky. Roughly 20,000 years ago, for instance, a Stone Age resident of what is now France sketched the moon's monthly phases on a cave wall. That drawing survives.

The artist and other members of his or her tribe likely wondered what that luminous sky object was. Perhaps one among them imagined rising from the ground and traveling to it. That dreamer may have wondered what the world he or she inhabited looked like from way up there. Maybe he or she devised the first story about a person flying into the sky.

Several ancient peoples had versions of just such a story. The ancient Greek one featured a brilliant craftsman and inventor, Daedalus. (His name came from a Greek word meaning "skillfully made.") The ruler of an island kingdom threw him and his young son, Icarus, into a prison cell. The two badly wanted to escape, and the cunning Daedalus came up with a plan. As the ancient Greek historian Diodorus Siculus told it, he "cleverly constructed wings fashioned in a marvelous manner and wonderfully held together by wax. When he had fastened these to his son's body and his own, he spread out his wings and escaped out over the sea." Just when it looked as if the getaway would be successful, however, tragedy struck. Because of his "youthful recklessness," Icarus flew too near the sun. The wax melted, and he fell into the sea and drowned.

This famous myth did not tell what Earth looked like to Icarus when he was flying near the sun. Perhaps the tale's earliest listeners pictured him gliding above and falling onto a large, flat disk. That is how many ancient peoples envisioned the world. Some saw that disk floating in an

immense sea. Others said the flat realm where humans lived was perched atop the back of a giant turtle or some other fanciful creature. The ancient Egyptians thought various gods stood on the Earth-disk and held up the sky.

The ancient Greeks came to reject such wrong-headed ideas about Earth's shape and place in the heavens. In the 500s BCE, the world's first scientists emerged in the Greek

In a Greek myth Icarus escaped from Crete with his father, Daedalus, but his wings melted when he flew too close to the sun.

The idea that the world is round soon became accepted throughout the lands surrounding the Mediterranean Sea.

lands. Nature is not controlled by supernatural beings and creatures, Thales, Pythagoras, and other Greek thinkers said. Instead, they proposed that the natural world is a mechanical system governed by logical laws.

One of those laws, they said, explained why celestial bodies are shaped like spheres. That included Earth, which they saw as being at the center of the cosmos. The idea that the world is round soon became accepted throughout the lands surrounding the Mediterranean Sea. Moreover, people did not merely accept this notion as a matter of faith. Greek thinkers offered evidence that they thought proved it.

The most renowned of those Greek scientists was Aristotle, who lived in the 300s BCE. One of the best proofs of a spherical Earth, he said, could easily be seen during lunar eclipses. An eclipse of the moon happens when Earth passes between the sun and moon. As the event progresses, Earth's shadow slowly moves across and covers the full moon's disk. In lunar eclipses, Aristotle wrote, Earth's "outline is always curved; and, since it is the [positioning] of the earth [between sun and moon] that makes the eclipse, the form of this line will be caused by the form of the earth's surface, which is therefore spherical."

Aristotle knew that the tale of Daedalus and Icarus was merely a myth and that people had never flown into the sky. What kept that from happening, he realized, was a natural force that held them and other objects firmly to

the ground. The Greeks did not call it gravity. But they recognized its existence and believed it to be an inherent quality that Earth possessed.

Aristotle did not write about human journeys beyond Earth, but some Greek and other ancient writers let their imaginations roam and did describe such journeys into the heavens. One was Lucian of Samosata, a Syrian who

As an early modern scientist, Kepler knew the approximate sizes of Earth and the moon.

wrote in Greek. He flourished in the 100s CE, when Rome controlled the Mediterranean world. His fanciful work, *A True Story,* describes a voyage to various heavenly bodies.

The narrative tells how the hero (Lucian himself) and a group of traveling companions were sucked into a giant waterspout. It "swept the ship round and up to a height of some three hundred and fifty miles above the Earth," Lucian wrote. The vessel was "suspended aloft, and at the same time carried along by a wind which struck and filled the sails." That wind carried the travelers to the moon. There the local ruler revealed that he was at war with the residents of the sun. The fight was over which of the two societies would gain possession of the planet Venus, called Lucifer in Lucian's book.

Lucian described what the voyagers saw as they descended toward their home world. First they passed Lampton, the realm of stars. Each was a small oil lamp that could think and talk. Moving lower, the travelers reached the clouds. From there, "we had a distinct view of the Ocean, though there was no land visible except the islands suspended in air."

A more scientific and realistic view of Earth from space appeared in a later tale of a trip to the moon. Titled *Somnium,* the work was written between 1609 and 1630 by the brilliant German astronomer Johannes Kepler. It is sometimes called the first modern science fiction story. As an early modern scientist, Kepler knew the approximate sizes of Earth and the moon. He also understood that the

smaller body revolves around the larger. In his story the moon people called their world Levania. And they referred to Earth as Volva. They see "Volva in the middle of their own sky," Kepler wrote. In the Levanian sky, Volva (Earth) has "a diameter a little less than four times longer than our moon to us." Thus, in comparing the two disks, "Volva's surface is fifteen times greater than our moon." These

figures are very close to the real ones, so Kepler may have added them to impart a feeling of authenticity. (Earth's diameter is 3.7 times the moon's, and the area of Earth's disk as seen from the moon is 13.5 times the moon's area as seen from Earth.)

The astronomers and other scientists who came after Kepler steadily increased human knowledge about the heavens. So stories about space travel became more and more realistic. *From the Earth to the Moon* (1865), by France's Jules Verne, was one of the most famous.

It depicts a spaceship shaped like a big bullet. A huge cannon fires it into space. Another was English writer H.G. Wells' *The First Men in the Moon* (1901). It tells the story of a trip from Earth to the moon by spaceship. A scientist and a businessman find the moon populated by insectlike creatures.

Only two years later, on December 17, 1903, two American inventors, Orville and Wilbur Wright, made history. At Kitty Hawk, North Carolina, Orville flew a flimsy little airplane that he and his brother Wilbur had pieced together. The flight lasted only 12 seconds and the plane went a mere 120 feet (37 meters). Yet the Wrights showed that heavier-than-air vehicles *could* fly.

These young men inspired many dreamers like themselves. Among them were other inventors, along with budding scientists and engineers. While some worked on building better airplanes, others turned their eyes and minds toward the heavens. They believed that if humans could fly from city to city in airplanes, they could also fly into space. Yet they knew that a major obstacle stood in the way of this goal. Escaping from Earth's gravity requires a craft to be very powerful and move extremely fast. And even the best airplanes lacked the necessary power and speed.

There was another flying device, however, that seemed to have the potential for travel beyond Earth—the rocket. One of the first scientists who suggested this use for rockets was an American, Robert Goddard. He knew that

They believed that if humans could fly from city to city in airplanes, they could also fly into space.

Robert Goddard's double-acting engine rocket was a major advance.

early rockets, like those used for fireworks, employed gunpowder for thrust. The problem was that gunpowder did not produce nearly enough sustained thrust. So he tried to create much more powerful liquid fuels. Goddard launched the first rocket powered by liquid fuel in 1926, and in the years that followed his rockets flew ever faster and higher.

German and Russian scientists experimented with rockets too. Some of the German versions were used as weapons during World War II. After that conflict Russian rocket scientists steadily caught up to those in the United States. As a result the Soviet Union (of which Russia was a part) was able to create a rocket powerful enough to carry an artificial satellite into orbit around Earth. It was *Sputnik 1* in 1957. A small, simple sphere that was primitive compared with later satellites, it had no camera to photograph Earth.

U.S. scientists and politicians were embarrassed that the Soviets had been first to put an object into Earth orbit. So the scientists worked overtime in hope of catching up. They placed the first U.S. satellite, *Explorer 1*, into orbit in 1958. The United States created an official space agency, NASA (the National Aeronautics and Space Administration), the same year. What was called a "space race" between the Americans and Soviets was now in full swing. It was understood that the winner would be the first nation to land a human being on the moon and bring him safely home.

In the *Friendship 7* capsule, John Glenn was the first American to orbit Earth.

In its efforts to beat the Soviets, NASA developed three manned space programs. Each was more complex than the one before it. The first was the Mercury program. It sent capsules carrying a single astronaut into near-Earth space—the region within a few hundred miles of the planet's surface. One Mercury astronaut, John Glenn, became the first American to orbit Earth, in February 1962. He snapped photos of the planet below. But at a maximum altitude of 162 miles (261 km), he was far too low to capture Earth's entire disk in a single shot.

The other two NASA programs designed to help put humans on the moon were called Gemini and Apollo. Two

Neil Armstrong, the first person to walk on the moon, took the iconic photo of his fellow astronaut Buzz Aldrin. *Life* magazine chose it as one of 100 photos that changed the world.

Apollo 11 was intended to carry out the first lunar landing. It accomplished that goal on July 20, 1969.

astronauts flew in each Gemini capsule, and three in each Apollo spacecraft. The mission of *Apollo 8,* which took the now famous Earthrise photo, was to test equipment while orbiting the moon. *Apollo 11* was intended to carry out the first lunar landing. It accomplished that goal on July 20, 1969. Astronaut Neil Armstrong climbed out of a lunar lander and set foot on the moon's surface. In doing so he capped an almost incredibly difficult achievement that only a few farsighted dreamers had envisioned over many centuries.

NASA quickly followed up with several more moon missions. *Apollos 12, 14, 15,* and *16* each put two astronauts on the lunar surface, where they conducted extensive experiments. (In each case the third man remained in the command module in lunar orbit. After leaving the surface, the lander rejoined the module and the three astronauts headed for home.) As it happened, the positions of Earth, the sun, and the spacecraft on these missions were never quite right to allow anyone to take a photo of a fully illuminated Earth. That special feat was accomplished by the astronauts aboard the program's final flight—*Apollo 17.*

The three men who share credit for creating the iconic Blue Marble photo came to NASA and the Apollo program by somewhat different routes. The mission's commander, Eugene Cernan, was born in Chicago in 1934. A good student in high school, he went on to earn college degrees in electrical and aeronautical engineering. His impressive

PALE BLUE DOT

Voyager 1 is 12 billion miles (19 billion km) from the sun.

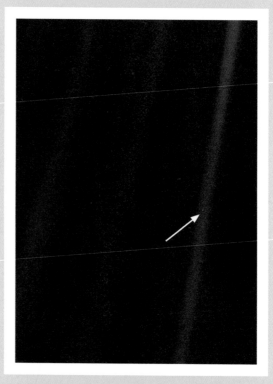

The blown-up picture of the Pale Blue Dot was taken through three color filters—violet, blue, and green—and recombined to produce the color image.

One of the most interesting of the many photos of Earth taken from space was created in 1990 by the unmanned *Voyager 1* spacecraft. *Voyager 1* and *2* were launched 16 days apart in 1977. Their mission was to fly by, study, and photograph the giant planets Jupiter and Saturn. After doing that, *Voyager 2* explored Uranus and Neptune, and both spacecraft continued on toward the solar system's outer regions.

Voyager 1 reached a point about 4 billion miles (6 billion km) from Earth on February 14, 1990. The onboard camera snapped a picture of the craft's home planet. At that great distance, Earth was so far away it looked like a tiny bluish-colored dot. So the image came to be known as Pale Blue Dot. In the photo a reflection off the spacecraft lights up the speck that is Earth in a beam of light.

"I still get chills down my back," said Candice Hansen-Koharcheck, years after the fact. She was the first person to see the image on her computer in NASA's Jet Propulsion Lab in California. "Because here was our planet, bathed in this ray of light, and it just looked incredibly special."

The twin Voyager spacecraft still send back scientific information and continue their mission to explore the far reaches of our solar system—and beyond. *Voyager 1* has entered interstellar space, the space between stars.

background persuaded NASA to accept him as an astronaut in 1963. Cernan served as the pilot of *Gemini 9* and flew on the *Apollo 10* mission before he was assigned to command *Apollo 17*. He became the 11th human to walk on the moon.

Ronald Evans, the mission's command module pilot, was born in St. Francis, Kansas, in 1933. Like Cernan,

he studied both electrical and aeronautical engineering before applying to be an astronaut. NASA accepted Evans in 1966. He served as backup command module pilot for *Apollo 14* before being chosen for *Apollo 17*.

Schmitt (left) and Cernan drive a lunar rover trainer in Nevada three months before the moon mission.

The third man aboard *Apollo 17*, Harrison "Jack" Schmitt, was born in Santa Rita, New Mexico, in 1935. He majored in science in college and earned a doctorate in geology. Late in 1964 NASA announced it wanted to recruit several astronauts who were also trained scientists. Of the more than 1,000 who applied, Schmitt was one of the six chosen. NASA assigned him to be the scientist aboard *Apollo 17*. The mission was to emphasize learning more about lunar geology, which made him especially valuable. He was scheduled to be the 12th person to walk on the moon.

As part of their extensive training for the mission, all three men learned to use the onboard cameras. They included 70-millimeter Hasselblads equipped with 80-mm lenses. The astronauts expected to take shots of all kinds of things, including their home planet. But they did not foresee that one of their pictures would become very possibly the most widely reproduced photo in history.

ChapterThree
AN ILLUMINATED GLOBE

Years of relentless, rigorous training were about to pay off for astronauts Eugene Cernan, Ronald Evans, and Jack Schmitt. Late in the afternoon of December 6, 1972, they began the complex process of donning their space suits. In the evening they made their way to the launch pad at the Kennedy Space Center.

As they approached, they could just make out the command module—the capsule they would ride in—sitting atop the enormous Saturn 5 rocket. The 363-foot- (111-m-) tall rocket looked like a giant pillar or a lofty skyscraper without windows. One observer called it "the most stupendous rocket ever built."

The three men had seen their share of majestic Saturns. They had watched them carry the previous Apollo crews aloft. But they knew that people seeing a Saturn in person for the first time were typically surprised and overwhelmed, finding it hard to believe that such an enormous object could get off the ground. The spectators who had gathered to watch the *Apollo 17* liftoff were about to witness the seemingly unbelievable.

The avid onlookers, whom some have affectionately called "space nuts," numbered an estimated half-million. Some had come from as far away as Maine and California, and even from foreign lands, to see the first night launch of an Apollo moon mission. They expected the liftoff to

One observer called it "the most stupendous rocket ever built."

The *Apollo 17* capsule sits atop the huge Saturn 5 rocket the night of the launch.

Apollo 17 is carried aloft during the first night launch in the lunar mission's history.

occur shortly before 10 p.m. But the countdown was suddenly halted. A tense two hours and 40 minutes elapsed while technicians found and corrected a minor mechanical problem.

Finally the countdown resumed. Inside the command module, Cernan, Evans, and Schmitt went through their final list of equipment checks. Before they knew it, the clock was at T-minus 20 seconds and counting.

The countdown slipped past 10 ... nine ... eight ... Suddenly the Saturn's mighty engines ignited. Immense clouds of glowing red-orange exhaust exploded outward

Only a few minutes after the launch, the three astronauts were orbiting high above their home planet.

from the launchpad's base. They lit up the plains and marshes for miles around.

The fantastic light show drew loud oohs and ahhs from the hundreds of thousands of spectators near the launch site. Their eyes remained riveted on the rocket as, like a massive fire-breathing creature, it began to climb into the dark sky at 12:33 a.m. Its rise seemed oddly slow at first. Clearly it was fighting hard to break free of Earth's strong gravitational pull. In a Herculean effort that sent a thrill of excitement through the watchers, it succeeded. Rapidly gaining speed and altitude, the flying skyscraper carried the *Apollo 17* crew skyward.

Eventually the Saturn workhorse's task of lifting the command module toward Earth orbit was finished. So it separated and fell away, leaving the capsule on its own. Only a few minutes after the launch, the three astronauts were orbiting high above their home planet.

As the capsule sped around Earth, the men busied themselves with a multitude of tasks. "There were a thousand critical things they had to do," explained Al Reinert, who made a documentary film about the Apollo program. They needed to "reorient and stabilize" the spacecraft, "check all the various systems and compute their [flight path], and climb out of the awkward hardsuits they'd been wearing since blast-off." Soon they would be leaving this parking orbit, in which they merely circled Earth over and over. At a preplanned moment, they would fire their thrusters and head for the mission's ultimate destination—the moon.

A view from
Apollo 17,
probably the
Indian Ocean east
of Madagascar

In the meantime, through their windows they could see
the planet's surface. It seemed to float by, steadily but sort
of lazily, below. Lakes, seas, and mountain ranges drifted
little by little from one horizon to another. The module
was not yet far enough away to glimpse and photograph
half of the globe in a single shot.

In fact, the men were not supposed to be snapping
photos at all at this point. Taking pictures was a job
that mission planners had scheduled for a few specific

moments in the voyage. Moreover, the astronauts had a limited amount of film for their cameras—12 color rolls and 11 black-and-white ones. These were intended to be used only during the preplanned photo sessions.

Finally, three hours and 12 minutes into the mission, all was ready. Cernan gave the order to fire the thrusters and leave orbit. The command module lurched, yanking the crew and their equipment in a new direction—toward the moon.

Again the astronauts busied themselves with chores for which they had trained long and hard. They were not supposed to be idly gazing out the windows. Yet "they couldn't help it," in Reinert's words. Today, he points out, the astronauts who went to the moon "talk most about and remember best the stolen moments of watching their home world shrink behind them." That "blue-green beacon in a vast black cosmos" seemed to beckon to them, forcing them to soak in the spectacular sight.

Slightly more than an hour and 50 minutes after the spacecraft had left orbit, the scene outside the windows grabbed at least one of the men's full attention. (Which of the three it was will likely never be known.) There, behind the module, floated planet Earth. This time the entire disk was fully illuminated by the sun—a sight seen extremely rarely by the occupants of NASA's spacecraft. As Reinert, the filmmaker, tells it, to see Earth this way "you need to pass through a point between it and the sun, which is a narrower window than you might think if you're traveling at 20,000 miles an hour. Most of the men who flew lunar missions saw neither a full Earth nor a full moon; both heavenly bodies were partly in shadow ... [during] the entire flight."

Earth, as seen at that moment from the *Apollo 17* module, free of the moon's shadow, was astonishingly bright and beautiful. At the top of the sunlit disk the Mediterranean Sea and nearly all of Africa's northern coast could be seen. To the right, the Arabian peninsula was clearly visible. Out to sea beyond it were the swirling clouds of a cyclone that had recently struck India. Also visible was the rest of the gigantic African continent, with the large island of Madagascar looming off its southeastern coast. As if adding frosting to the visual cake, much of the ice-covered continent of Antarctica could be seen along the disk's bottom edge.

That "blue-green beacon in a vast black cosmos" seemed to beckon to them, forcing them to soak in the spectacular sight.

Earth, the Blue Marble, as viewed from *Apollo 17*

There was no doubt that a photo needed to be taken of this exceptional sight. Whoever thought to do it reached for the only Hasselblad camera that was not packed away and snapped four shots roughly a minute apart. The second one would prove to be the sharpest and clearest.

A LONG-RUNNING FEUD

Eugene Cernan (left) and Harrison Schmitt inside the Apollo 17 *command module*

All three *Apollo 17* astronauts snapped at least a few photos of Earth from the command module during the flight. Partly for that reason, each of the men later came to believe that he had snapped the Blue Marble image. Ronald Evans still seemed to hold that opinion at the time of his death in 1990.

But throughout the 40-some years following the mission, Cernan and Schmitt continued to stake their own claims to the famous photo. As filmmaker Al Reinert says, the Blue Marble turned out "to be the most significant thing they brought back from their expedition." It was "far more meaningful than the moon

rocks they gathered, so it matters to them." As a result, the two men developed a running feud over the matter.

Their disagreement was evident at an event staged in 2002 to observe the 30th anniversary of the *Apollo 17* mission. Filmmaker James Cameron organized a fancy dinner at a Los Angeles mansion, Reinert explains. "A limousine was dispatched to fetch Cernan and Schmitt from their hotel. Schmitt grabbed it first and told the driver to get moving, stranding Cernan and his wife. After the dinner Cernan returned the insult by stranding Schmitt and his wife. They won't even ride in the same stretch limo together."

No doubt the man who created the image did not realize then how famous it would become. He did not say anything to Mission Control about taking the picture. Nor did he mention it to his crewmates. Most experts suppose that he became busy with more pressing tasks and stopped thinking about the photos he had taken.

None of the *Apollo 17* crewmen said anything about what came to be called the Blue Marble photo until a film technician mentioned it a couple of weeks later. That man, Dick Underwood, processed the mission's film in a NASA lab. Seeing the second, very sharp shot of the fully lit Earth, he immediately brought it to the attention of NASA officials, and they released it to the news media. Soon the image was reproduced in newspapers and magazines around the globe.

Only then did the true uniqueness and importance of the photo become plain to the three astronauts. Each spoke about it in later months and years, giving it his own individual spin. Cernan summed up its emotional impact particularly well. "Do you know where you are at this point in time and space, and in reality and in existence, when you can look out the window and you're looking at the most beautiful star in the heavens?" he asked in an interview. "The most beautiful because it's the one we understand and we know, it's home, it's people, family, love, life—and besides that it is beautiful. You can see from pole to pole and across oceans and continents and you can watch it turn and there's no strings holding it up, and it's moving in a blackness that is almost beyond conception."

Soon the image was reproduced in newspapers and magazines around the globe.

Chapter Four

A WORLD WITHOUT BORDERS

The legacy of the Blue Marble is enormous. That single photo soon came to outshine the mission's many other achievements, some of which were noteworthy. For example, the crew was the first of all the astronauts NASA sent into space to include a professional scientist (geologist Harrison Schmitt). "*Apollo 17* was arguably the most scientifically oriented mission to the moon," NBC News science editor Alan Boyle points out. It "helped set the precedent for research" on such later NASA projects as "the space shuttle and the International Space Station."

The *Apollo 17* astronauts brought back more rocks, soil, and other moon samples than had any of the other lunar missions. Among the samples was the first orange-colored dirt ever discovered on the moon. Scientists found that it was composed of thousands of tiny glass beads. They had been formed from lava ejected during lunar volcanic eruptions more than 3 billion years ago.

But these and the mission's other accomplishments almost faded into obscurity as a result of the Blue Marble's spectacular rise to fame. Seeing the planet suspended in space, alone yet majestic against the black canopy of the cosmos, seized people's imaginations. The photo "is often credited with changing the way people think about our planet," atmospheric scientist Donald Wuebbles remarked.

The photo "is often credited with changing the way people think about our planet."

Harrison Schmitt uses an adjustable scoop to retrieve lunar samples.

The vast majority of Earthlings take the ground beneath their feet for granted. To them, Earth is simply where they and millions of other species live and thrive. The idea that the surfaces of all the other planets in our solar system do not support life may seem strange and hard to grasp. The Blue Marble clearly shows the telltale signs of life on Earth, visual hints missing from images of other planetary disks. These signs, NASA says, include our world's "blue expanse of ocean, its thin yet dynamic veil of atmosphere, and its brown and green jigsaw of continents all give Earth a vitality unknown anywhere else in the universe."

Seeing Earth this way frequently stimulates emotional responses in those who have studied the photo. Astronaut Alan Shepard Jr., who commanded the *Apollo 14* mission, admitted to expressing such emotions during that expedition: "If somebody'd said before the flight, 'Are you going to get carried away looking at the Earth from the moon?' I would have [said], 'No, no way.' But yet when I first looked back at the Earth, standing on the moon, I cried."

Ben Cosgrove, editor of Life.com, makes the same point. "No other photograph ever made of planet Earth," he wrote, "has ever felt at-once so momentous and somehow so manageable, so *companionable*, as 'Blue Marble.'"

It is natural to consider why the picture has become so appealing to people worldwide. One reason cited by many people is that it shows a world without national or other borders. Although such boundaries are needed in some ways, they can be divisive. It has been said that the Blue Marble serves as a reminder that all the planet's residents are neighbors and to various degrees dependent on one another.

Describing his experience on the *Apollo 9* mission, astronaut Russell Schweickart said, "When you go around the Earth in an hour and half, you begin to recognize that your identity is with the whole thing. And that makes a change. You look down there and you can't imagine how many borders and boundaries you cross, again and again

"But yet when I first looked back at the Earth, standing on the moon, I cried."

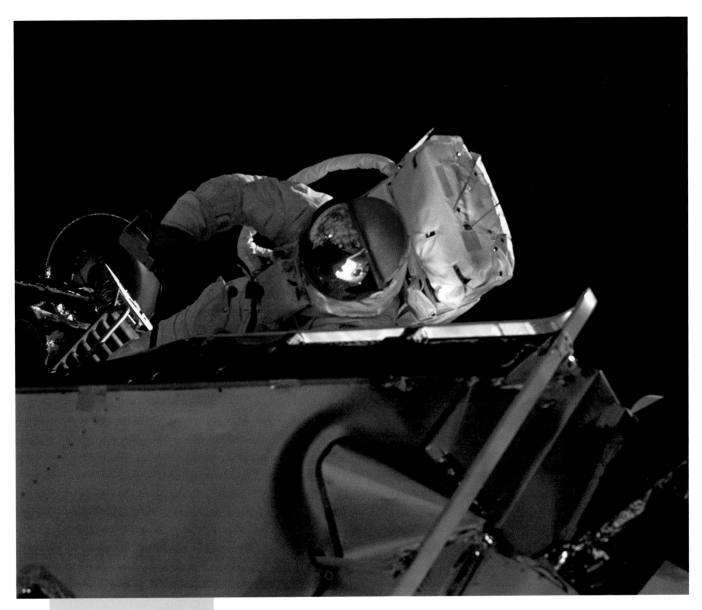

Russell Schweickart retrieves a thermal sample during the *Apollo 9* mission.

and again, and you don't even see them. ... And from where you see it, the thing is a whole, the earth is a whole, and it's so beautiful. You wish you could take a person in each hand, one from each side in the various conflicts, and say, 'Look. Look at it from this perspective. Look at that. What's important?'"

The Blue Marble image is often associated with Earth Day, including adorning a flag in 1989.

"I was not alone in feeling that the photograph evoked how beautiful, fragile, and unique our home is and how important it is to understand and preserve it."

Another important reason for the Blue Marble's widespread appeal is the insight and inspiration it has given to those who care about the environment and work to protect it. For them, the image cautions humanity that its home in the dark cosmic wilderness is small and frail and therefore needs to be protected and nurtured. The scientist Donald Wuebbles sums it up well: "I was not alone in feeling that the photograph evoked how beautiful, fragile, and unique our home is and how important it is to understand and preserve it. Seeing for the first time 'our' 'Blue Marble' in a vast void has brought home to many how much we depend on the Earth and that it is our responsibility to protect the health and well-being of this collective, interdependent ecosystem. So it is not surprising that the 'Blue Marble' became the symbol of the environmental movement that had started with the first Earth Day [in 1970]."

The Blue Marble's ability to touch the minds and hearts of so many people around the globe has had many cultural consequences. The image has been used to represent or advertise a staggering array of organizations and products, both commercial and nonprofit. It has appeared in print ads and TV commercials for cars, power tools, computer games, and potato chips, to name only a few. It has also shown up in wallpaper for computer monitors, mouse pad designs, and illustrations in books, magazines, and newspapers, as well as on T-shirts, billboards, and book covers, including Greg Bear's science fiction novel *Eon*.

A U.S. postage stamp featured the Blue Marble in 1999.

The Blue Marble image is well-known for its appearances on environmental posters. The text on one popular poster reads: "Believed to be unique, this magnificent dwelling has been sadly neglected in recent years. Some outstanding features have been lost. However it still offers an exceptional home to those prepared to maintain it with care."

Perceptive film buffs noticed still another use of the Blue Marble in director Ron Howard's 1995 movie,

THE BLACK MARBLE

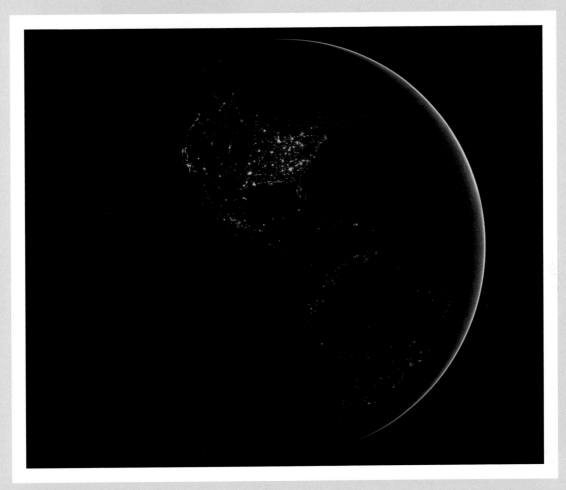

Data for the night view was acquired over nine days during 312 orbits to get a clear shot of every part of Earth.

NASA has created a series of nighttime views of Earth from space, calling the collection the Black Marble. Taken by the Visible Infrared Imaging Radiometer Suite and released in December 2012, the images show a delicate network of city lights across the world.

"The night is nowhere as dark as most of us think," said Steven Miller, a Colorado State University atmospheric scientist. "In fact, the Earth is never really dark. And we don't have to be in the dark about what is happening at night anymore either."

Using the nighttime images is proving very helpful to experts in several fields. Among them are demographers, who study human population growth and changes. From observing patterns of city lights at night, they can tell which areas of the country and the world have the most concentrated, as well as the most sparse, settlements.

Astronomers are also keen on the Black Marble photos. By examining them, they can select the darkest regions of the continents. This helps them plan where to build observatories, which need to be as far as possible from light pollution.

The Black Marble pictures also give electric companies a way to monitor the occurrence of power blackouts.

The Western Hemisphere view of Blue Marble 2012

Apollo 13. The film told the suspenseful story of the only Apollo moon mission that had to be scrubbed in mid-flight because of an onboard malfunction. Some viewers have complained that the movie used the image too often. The filmmakers "used this photograph of Earth so many times I lost count," said software engineer Neil Fraser. "Every time the crew looked out the window, there was Africa and Antarctica. Obviously Earth doesn't spin in this movie."

Besides the seemingly countless copies of the Blue Marble image distributed over the years, the picture

has lent its name to other photographic projects with similar themes. One of the better known examples is Blue Marble 2012, which NASA calls the "most amazing high definition image of Earth." It is a composite image that "uses a number of swaths of the Earth's surface taken on January 4, 2012."

The composite shot of the Western Hemisphere, showing North, Central, and South America, was released January 25, 2012. A companion photo of the Eastern Hemisphere, showing Africa, Saudi Arabia, and India, appeared a few days later. The images were taken by a new instrument, the Visible Infrared Imaging Radiometer Suite, which was flying aboard a research satellite, the Suomi National Polar-orbiting Partnership.

Another famous Blue Marble-like image, released by NASA in 2002, is a popular default wallpaper image for the iPhone.

One of the most striking aspects of the Blue Marble image and its many copies and spin-offs is that they all deal with Earth in some way, not with the moon. The *Apollo 17* astronauts did not foresee that they would create a widely famous picture of their home planet. They did not anticipate that they would produce perhaps the most often copied photographic image in history. Instead they and their predecessors' attention was riveted on the moon and what they could learn about it.

As NASA astronaut Bill Anders, creator of the famous Earthrise photo, remarked, "I've always used the phrase, 'ironic.' We came all this way to discover the moon. And what we really did discover is Earth."

Apollo 17 astronauts captured Earth shining in the distance above the lunar surface.

Timeline

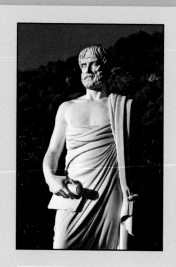

c. 625 BCE

Birth of Thales, the first Greek thinker known to have proposed that the cosmos is a mechanical system governed by natural laws

384 BCE

Birth of Aristotle, a Greek scholar, teacher, and thinker who, among other achievements, presented evidence that Earth is round

c. 160 CE

Lucian, a Syrian writing in Greek, publishes a story about a trip to the moon

1901

British writer H.G. Wells publishes his novel *First Men in the Moon*

1903

American inventors Orville and Wilbur Wright achieve the first flight of a heavier-than-air vehicle, an airplane

c. 1609–1630

German astronomer Johannes Kepler writes *Somnium,* about a moon voyage

1865

French writer Jules Verne publishes *From the Earth to the Moon*

1926

American inventor Robert Goddard launches the first rocket that uses liquid fuel

1957

The Soviets put the first human-made satellite, *Sputnik 1,* in orbit

Timeline

1958

The United States launches its first satellite, *Explorer 1*

1959

The Soviets' *Luna 2* successfully crash-lands on the moon

1961

Vostok 1 carries Soviet cosmonaut Yuri Gagarin into orbit; he becomes the first human in space

1969

The *Apollo 11* mission lands the first people on the moon

1972

The *Apollo 17* astronauts snap the shot of Earth in space that will soon become known as the iconic Blue Marble

1962

John Glenn becomes the first American to orbit Earth

1968

The *Apollo 8* spacecraft orbits the moon and takes the famous photo called Earthrise, which shows Earth floating above the lunar horizon

1990

The *Voyager 1* spacecraft takes a photo of the distant Earth, an image that will become known as Pale Blue Dot

2012

NASA releases a collection of nighttime views called the Black Marble and Blue Marble 2012, high-definition composite images of Earth

Glossary

celestial: relating to the stars and the sky

command module: the crew's quarters and flight-control section of an Apollo spacecraft

cosmos: the universe

demographer: scientist who studies the growth and density of populations and their vital statistics

environmental: relating to the natural world and the impact of human activity on its condition

geologist: scientist who studies how Earth formed and how it changes, by examining soil, rocks, rivers, and other landforms

gibbous: seen with more than half but not all of a disk lighted

iconic: widely viewed as perfectly capturing the meaning or spirit of something or someone

lunar: having to do with the moon

panorama: a very wide, sweeping view or scene

solar system: the sun and all the planets, moons, comets, and smaller bodies orbiting it

sophisticated: developed to a high degree of complexity

vulnerable: exposed to the possibility of being attacked or harmed

Additional Resources

Further Reading

Carlisle, Rodney P. *Exploring Space*.
New York: Chelsea House, 2010.

Green, Carl. *Spacewalk: The Astounding Gemini 4 Mission*.
Berkeley Heights, N.J.: Enslow Publishers, 2013.

Nardo, Don. *Destined for Space: Our Story of Exploration*.
Smithsonian. North Mankato, Minn.: Capstone Press, 2012.

Space: A Visual Encyclopedia. New York: DK Publishing, 2010.

Internet Sites

Use FactHound to find Internet sites related
to this book. All of the sites on FactHound
have been researched by our staff.

Here's all you do:
Visit *www.facthound.com*
Type in this code: 9780756547325

Critical Thinking Using the Common Core

What evidence did the ancient Greek scholar Aristotle offer to show that people could not fly into the sky? (Key Ideas and Details)

Read the sidebar on page 42. Why do you think the question of who took the Blue Marble photo led to such a long-standing feud? How might you have resolved the conflict? (Integration of Knowledge and Ideas)

What are three ways that experts in various fields have benefited from the Black Marble collection of nighttime views of Earth? (Key Ideas and Details)

Source Notes

Page 4, line 1: Alan Boyle, science editor. "40 years later, *Apollo 17*'s Blue Marble leaves a mark on our memory." NBC News. 7 Dec. 2012. 2 Oct. 2013. http://cosmiclog.nbcnews.com/_news/2012/12/07/15755286-40-years-later-apollo-17s-blue-marble-leaves-a-mark-on-our-memory?lite

Page 9, line 1: Mike Wall. "*Apollo 17*, 40 years later: 'I treasure the whole mission.'" NBC News. 12 July 2012. 2 Oct. 2013.http://www.nbcnews.com/id/50118480/ns/technology_and_science-space/#.UUSD9leRfDS

Page 10, line 4: "The genesis of *Apollo 8*'s 'earthrise.'" NBC News. 15 July 1999. 2 Oct. 2013. http://www.nbcnews.com/id/3077909/#.UUSnhVeRfDQ

Page 11, line 21: "40 Years Later, *Apollo 17*'s Blue Marble leaves a mark on our memory."

Page 13, line 6: Gregory A. Petsko. "The Blue Marble." *Genome Biology*. Vol. 12(4); 2011. 2 Oct. 2013. U.S. National Library of Medicine, National Institutes of Health. http://www.ncbi.nlm.nih.gov/pmc/articles/PMC3218853/

Page 17, line 15: Diodorus Siculus. *Library of History*, excerpted in Rhoda A. Hendricks, editor and translator, *Classical Gods and Heroes: Myths as Told by the Ancient Authors*. New York: Morrow Quill, 1974, pp. 104–105.

Page 19, line 20: Aristotle. *On the Heavens*, translated by J.L. Stocks, Book II, part 14. The Internet Classics Archive. http://classics.mit.edu/Aristotle/heavens.2.ii.html

Page 21, line 6: *The Works of Lucian of Samosata*, translated by H.W. and F.G. Fowler, digital copyright 2012, p. 226. http://books.google.com/books?id=NNM43hFTURwC&printsec=frontcover&dq=The+works+of+lucian+of+Samosata&hl=en&sa=X&ei=NtbBUfvIB6784AON3YGAAg&ved=0CDUQ6AEwAQGAAg&ved=0CDUQ6AEwAQ

Page 21, line 19: Ibid., p. 230.

Page 22, line 3: Johannes Kepler. *Somnium*, translated by Norman R. Faladeau. Frosty Dew Observatory and Sky Theatre. 2 Oct. 2013. http://frostydrew.org/papers.dc/papers/paper-somnium/

Page 30, col. 2, line 4: Nell Greenfieldboyce. "An Alien View of Earth." *All Things Considered*. NPR. 12 Feb. 2010. 2 Oct. 2013. http://www.npr.org/2010/02/12/123614938/an-alien-view-of-earth

Page 34, line 11: Al Reinert. "The Blue Marble Shot: Our First Complete Photograph of Earth." *The Atlantic*. 12 April 2011. 2 Oct. 2013. http://www.theatlantic.com/technology/archive/2011/04/the-blue-marble-shot-our-first-complete-photograph-of-earth/237167/

Page 37, line 19: Ibid.

Page 39, line 12: Ibid.

Page 40, line 10: Ibid.

Page 42, line 10:Ibid.

Page 42, col. 2, line 6: Ibid.

Page 43, line 20: Donald J.Wuebbles. "Celebrating the 'Blue Marble.'" *EOS, Transactions, American Geophysical Union*. Vol. 93, No. 49, p. 511. 4 Dec. 2012. 2 Oct. 2013. http://elearning.lsgi.org/GUR/test/Celebrating%20Blue%20Marble.pdf

Page 44, line 6: "40 years later, *Apollo 17*'s Blue Marble leaves a mark on our memory."

Page 44, line 23: "Celebrating the 'Blue Marble.'"

Page 45, line 9: "Planet Earth." *National Geographic*. 3 July 2013. 2 Oct. 2013. http://science.nationalgeographic.com/science/space/solar-system/earth/

Page 46, line 5: International Space Hall of Fame at the New Mexico Museum of Space History. 2 Oct. 2013. http://www.nmspacemuseum.org/halloffame/detail.php?id=55

Page 46, line 11: Ben Cosgrove. "Home, Sweet Home: In Praise of 'Blue Marble.'" Life.com. 2 Oct. 2013. http://life.time.com/history/blue-marble-the-iconic-apollo-17-photo-of-earth-from-space-turns-40/#1

Page 46, line 24: Russell Schweickart. "No Frames, No Boundaries: Connecting with the whole planet—from space," in *Rediscovering the North American Vision*. Summer 1983. 2 Oct. 2013. http://www.context.org/iclib/ic03/schweick/

Page 49, line 7: "Celebrating the 'Blue Marble,'" p. 510.

Page 50, line 3: Neil Fraser. "The One, the Only Photograph of Earth." March 2001. 2 Oct. 2013. http://neil.fraser.name/writing/earth/

Page 51, line 6: Michael Carlowicz. "Out of the Blue and Into the Black." NASA Earth Observatory. 5 Dec. 2012. 3 July 2013. http://earthobservatory.nasa.gov/Features/IntotheBlack/

Page 52, line 5: "The One, the Only Photograph of Earth."

Page 53, line 3: "Most Amazing High Definition Image of Earth—Blue Marble 2012." 25 Jan. 2012. 2 July 2013. http://www.flickr.com/photos/gsfc/6760135001/

Page 54, line 18: Ron Judd. "With a view from beyond the moon, an astronaut talks religion, politics and possibilities." *The Seattle Times*. 7 Dec. 2012. 2 Oct. 2013. http://seattletimes.com/html/pacificnw/2019783643_pacificpanders09.html

Select Bibliography

"The Apollo Program." Smithsonian Institution. http://airandspace.si.edu/collections/imagery/apollo/AS17/a17.htm

Boyle, Alan. "40 Years Later, *Apollo 17*'s Blue Marble leaves a mark on our memory." NBC News. http://cosmiclog.nbcnews.com/_news/2012/12/07/15755286-40-years-later-apollo-17s-blue-marble-leaves-a-mark-on-our-memory?lite

Cernan, Eugene, and Don Davis. *Last Man on the Moon: Astronaut Eugene Cernan and America's Race in Space.* New York: St. Martin's Press, 1999.

Chaikin, Andrew. *A Man on the Moon: The Voyages of the Apollo Astronauts.* New York: Penguin, 2007.

Collins, Michael. *Carrying the Fire: An Astronaut's Journeys.* New York: Farrar, Straus, and Giroux, 2009.

Cosgrove, Ben. "Home, Sweet Home: In Praise of 'Blue Marble.'" Life.com. http://life.time.com/history/blue-marble-the-iconic-apollo-17-photo-of-earth-from-space-turns-40/#1

Fraser, Neil. "The One, the Only Photograph of Earth." http://neil.fraser.name/writing/earth/

"The Genesis of Apollo 8's 'Earthrise.'" NBC News. http://www.nbcnews.com/id/3077909/#.UUSnhVeRfDQ

Hope, Terry. *Spacecam: Photographing the Final Frontier, from Apollo to Hubble.* Devon, England: David and Charles, 2007.

Kelly, Thomas J. *Moon Lander: How We Developed the Apollo Lunar Module.* Washington, D.C.: Smithsonian Institution Press, 2009.

Kluger, Jeffrey. "Earth from Above: The Blue Marble." *Time.* http://lightbox.time.com/2012/02/09/blue-marble/#1

Petsko, Gregory A. "The Blue Marble." *Genome Biology.* Vol. 12(4); 2011. U.S. National Library of Medicine, National Institutes of Health. http://www.ncbi.nlm.nih.gov/pmc/articles/PMC3218853/

Reinert, Al. "The Blue Marble Shot: Our First Complete Photograph of Earth." *The Atlantic.* 12 April 2011. http://www.theatlantic.com/technology/archive/2011/04/the-blue-marble-shot-our-first-complete-photograph-of-earth/237167/

Wall, Mike. "'*Apollo 17*, 40 years later: 'I treasure the whole mission.'" NBC News. 12 July 2012. http://www.nbcnews.com/id/50118480/ns/technology_and_science-space/#.UUSD9leRfDS

Wall, Mike. "Giant Leaps: Top Milestones of Human Spaceflight." Space.com. http://www.space.com/11329-human-spaceflight-biggest-moments-50th-anniversary.html

U.S. Geological Survey. "Harrison H. Schmitt." http://astrogeology.usgs.gov/rpif/harrison-h-schmitt

Wuebbles, Donald J. "Celebrating the 'Blue Marble.'" *EOS, Transactions, American Geophysical Union.* Vol. 93, No. 49, p. 511. 4 Dec. 2012. http://elearning.lsgi.org/GUR/test/Celebrating%20Blue%20Marble.pdf

Zimmerman, Robert. *Genesis: The Story of Apollo 8: The First Manned Flight to Another World.* New York: Random House Publishing Group, 2000.

Index

About the Author

Historian and award-winning author Don Nardo has written many books for young people about astronomy, the planets, extraterrestrial life, and other topics relating to outer space. Nardo lives with his wife, Christine, in Massachusetts.